UFO

A MESSAGE FROM THE PLEIADES

AGUSTÍN OSORNIO

All rights reserved. The total or partial reproduction of this work is not allowed, nor its incorporation into a computer system, or its transmission in any form or by any means (electronic, mechanical, photocopying, recording, or otherwise) without the prior written permission of the copyright holder is a violation of these rights and may constitute a crime against intellectual property

The content of this work is the responsibility of the author and does not necessarily reflect the views of the publishing house. All texts and images were provided by the author, who is solely responsible for their rights.

Published by Ibukku, LLC
www.ibukku.com
Graphic Design: Diana Patricia González J.
Cover Design: Ángel Flores Guerra B.
Copyright © 2023
ISBN Paperback: 978-1-68574-402-1
ISBN eBook: 978-1-68574-403-8

Author's Notes

It is certainly difficult for people to believe in the existence of contact with extraterrestrial beings, however, my personal experience shows that we are not alone, that in the universe there are beings of greater intelligence than us and whose technological advance is thousands of years old. They are beings who seek social stability and independence from the yoke of corrupt governments.

For all human beings who have been contacted, experience shows us that there is someone behind an entire creation:

God, who within his infinite wisdom and love points out to us that we are not alone in the universe, that humans are not the only intelligent beings, inhabitants of other stars have been coexisting with us since ancient times, but unfortunately, there were cataclysms and earthquakes that destroyed continents and lives, leaving valuable information in the dark.

It is true that little could be rescued, like what Plato wrote, and people took it as mythology, but in this book, I will show you the truth according to the information that my extraterrestrial brothers have shared with me. They have been helping me communicate to all those who are looking forward to, not only the extraterrestrial phenomenon but also the prophecies of the Mayans and the Aztec calendar, which indicate that from the year 2012, a change occurred on our planet, events that were already written in the Bible.

In this book, I will tell you how extraterrestrial contact changed my life, even though many made fun of me, ignored me; calling me "stupid" and others "lunatic." Thanks to a person who called me "ignorant," I was able to look up in the dictionary the meaning of that word and it was then that I felt motivated to write this work asking my extraterrestrial brothers for help and intelligence, especially my teacher Higer. This last one showed me that being humble, patient, and listening with an immense desire not only got me to get out of my ignorance but also to grow spiritually. He taught wonderful things that millions of people would have liked to know, I am not only talking about the wisdom and intelligence of such beings who shared that information with me and to whom I appreciate that you have shown me the love of God not according to human judgment, but I also refer to the infinite wisdom of God.

I hope that this story is to your liking and that each one of you can make sense of it according to your criteria. This message brings peace and hope that human beings have not been able to find in a world where we currently live in a decadent society in which lack of morality, selfishness, and lack of faith, and where people do not believe in a loving and compassionate God. His message is for you and through this, God calls you not to lose trust in Him.

Dedications

To God the Father and to his son Jesus Christ,
for all the great miracles and favors received.

To my wife and daughters, who were patient
with me so that I could dedicate myself to this work.

To my friends, who gave me their unconditional
support and motivation to be able to finish this book.

To my daughter Vanessa Osornio, who helped me design the cover.

Introduction

In February 1976 my life changed forever. We all dream of being able to fulfill ourselves, by achieving goals and purposes to be able to live in a better world, but what happened to me gave me more than a change, a different way of thinking, to see beyond our horizon, knowing that there is life on other planets and noticing that the universe is as immense as the love of God.

I will try to write according to what my extraterrestrial or Pleiadian brothers showed me so that I could share their message with humanity. I am not a writer; the message was written in accordance with my experience. Any similarities to other writers or people who have experienced similar circumstances are because each contactee is part of a universal message that contains a great truth that we cannot hide or ignore; itself, the researchers or followers of the extraterrestrial phenomenon give much to think because of the way each of the contactees has been "abducted."

The Pleiadians are bringing us closer to a "cosmic" consciousness to which the human being needs to wake up to see beyond his own horizon, and also I affirm I'm still in contact with them, humans are limited to a negative way of thinking that supposes that within this immense universe, we men are the only ones who have life and intelligence. It makes me laugh to see how much Governments like historians manipulate or hide information to be able to submerge human beings within ignorance.

Today the time has come to show planet Earth that extraterrestrial beings have always been within the course of humanity and that each of us has been part of experiments with highly advanced biogenetics from which we must discern that we are pieces of a divine plan of procreation, but not of evolution, according to stupid "investigations" that are arrogant and that irritate the wrath of our Creator.

My present book will lead you to have more information about what extraterrestrial contact meant, and how it changed the course of my life; will also boldly maintain that it is ridiculous and insolent to say that we are the only intelligent beings in the universe, setting aside our Divine Creator, whatever his name is; "I am who I am."

April 2007, City of Los Angeles, CA.

*I*t's half past eight in the morning and I find myself doing my work; I am a class A driver and my task is to move containers from the train to the lots. My name is Agustín, but all my friends know me as "UFO" or "the Extraterrestrial"; the truth is that everyone makes jokes about whether I have seen UFOs or aliens and they try to joke around on the radio about the phenomenon. The truth is that it doesn't bother me. I had been working for the company for nine years and I have gotten used to it; as a joke, I answered, them back taking what they said to me as well. The first to make a comment is the one we call "Pelón"; he tells me on the radio:

"Hey, UFO, did you know that they just discovered water on the red planet, Mars?"

"Of course, I do, I know it, but that water isn't for drinking," I told him.

"Why?" The Baldhead asked.

"Because the aliens who go there are going to relieve themselves passing through that planet," I told him.

The laughter of all my friends can be heard on the radio causing a big fuss; my supervisor calls my attention telling me that it is forbidden to use bad language on the radio and asks me to go talk to the Terminal

Manager. I go with my truck to the offices and there is my supervisor, who has known me for a long time. He tells his superior that everyone jokes with me and that is why I answered with that tone of voice on the radio.

My terminal manager is called Kyile, and he asks my supervisor to leave so he can talk to me alone, so he tells me, "I've wanted to talk to you about the extraterrestrial phenomenon for a long time. Let's forget about the incident for now, I want to share with you the experience of an encounter I had." I paid attention to him and he told me that he had also seen UFOs, that he could give credit to what he had observed and that from there he had great concern about such a phenomenon, but he did not dare to mention it to no one because others might think he might be "crazy or on drugs." When he finished telling me about his personal experience, he asked me if what he had seen was true or if it had been a product of his imagination. I replied, "Look, Kyile, according to my personal experience I can tell you that it is ridiculous to think that we are alone in the universe," and I told him that National Geographic had published an article on astronomy that made reference to the fact that in our galaxy the Milky Way is home to a number of approximately 10,000 suns similar to ours, which they are medium G-type stars according to their age and characteristics within astronomical spectrum studies. That means that we are certainly not alone in the universe as there may be stars that have developed intelligent life. On the other hand, there are more stars where there is life much more advanced than ours.

I began to touch on the subject of where the intelligent beings who had coincidentally contacted me had come from and what had been their purpose in visiting Earth and coming into personal contact with us. Kyile was looking at me absorbed, without interrupting me, and suddenly he said why don't you tell me about your personal experience, we went out after our work hours, "While you talk to me, I'll buy you lunch." So we *did and that same afternoon we arrived at a restaurant and after eating I prepared to narrate what happened 31 years ago.*

It all happened in Mexico City, it was in February 1976... At that time I was 22 years old and single; I had a business that in the United States they call it a minimarket. Throughout my work time, I was always busy attending to my business, which several times prevented me from socializing or having many friends, everything was the same routine as always, but I allowed myself to have a very stable income and live not in luxury but in a comfortable way. It was already closing time, twelve o'clock at night, and I had to drive a distance of 20 to 25 minutes; the house was located in a residential area called Lomas Estrella and precisely near there is the Cerro de la Estrella, which is very famous for being the place where the Passion and Death are celebrated every year of our Lord Jesus Christ.

It was already half past twelve at night and I was about to open the garage, I had to park the car outside the curb to be able to open the doors and, since the streets in Mexico are very narrow, I had to put on my flashers to prevent other cars from hitting me while I parked my vehicle. Suddenly, I intuitively fixed my gaze on the houses on the hill and I was able to observe a grey oval metallic object, but with a very bright light of its own. The light was so strong you could see the little houses, their diameter was approximately 20 feet high by 80 feet long. It was a UFO lab for which I could notice perfectly; He moved slowly from one place to another. I was amazed, I could not believe what my eyes had seen. In my mind, I asked myself a thousand questions: from where and how is it that he was there and why. I was watching him for 20 minutes, but I was so tired that I parked the car, took a bath, and smoked a cigarette to sleep comfortably, according to my custom.

That night nothing happened.

The next morning I woke up at the same time to go open the business. Thus the whole day passed, and at midnight—as it was customary—I closed the business. Once at home, I went to bed to enjoy my cigarette, when suddenly a very intense precious sky blue light was projected in my room; the light blinded me. I was very excited and surprised, I couldn't believe what was happening, I tried to sit up in bed but a force did not allow me to move; I thought, "What could that be?"

Suddenly I felt that they were holding me strongly but without hurting me, I tried to move but I couldn't, I tried to speak to warn my parents but I couldn't say a word and I thought to myself, "Who are you?" but they did not answer me.

I think everything changed when I told them in my thoughts, "It's fine, I wish to cooperate," and they released my body, which I experienced laxity and rest so great that I felt as if I were dead, an enormous peace, something that I had never felt in my life. Then soon I heard in my mind that someone was speaking to me and saying, "Rest, don't be afraid, we won't hurt you," and I mentally told them that I was fine, that I felt comfortable; there was no pain or concern, nothing bad existed. I could only see three silhouettes, the light was too intense, and I could only appreciate their bodies. Two were the size of a child and the other body was about two meters high. Suddenly I fell into a deep sleep as if I had been anesthetized, I don't know how much time passed; when the precious blue light slowly disappeared from my bedroom, I jumped from my bed and I didn't see anyone. I said to myself, "This was not a dream." I could not put out the cigarette because it was on my bedside folded table as if they had turned it off because the smoke bothered them or perhaps they did not like the smell. I always finished my cigarette and that time it was halfway through and folded. The blinds were half closed, I never left them like this because the street light pole was in front of my bedroom and yes I drew the curtains far down so the light would not hit my face. I had one and a thousand questions but I couldn't find an explanation at that moment. My watch stopped at that moment, everything was confusing to me, and perhaps my fatigue and long working hours also played a role.

I got ready to sleep and the next morning I told my parents what happened. They stood looking at each other as if to say what I have had; my dad asked me,

"Son, what did you smoke or what did you drink?"

"Dad, Mom, you know from my long working hours that I'm not allowed to socialize with my friends," I replied.

After telling them what happened, they did not believe me. After lunch time passed and before I went back to the business, while my sister was in charge, I noticed something very curious because I felt itchy and I saw that my heels had something like a prick of mosquitoes and I told myself that it was not possible for a mosquito to do this because the mark had made a perfectly rounded shape one on each side, that wasn't a coincidence. Then I remembered what happened the night before and I thought, "Have the aliens done something to me?" I could not stop questioning myself. I went back to my business and put alcohol on it and noticed that those marks spit oozed out a whitish substance, but I didn't feel any pain so I went back to work. That night my life changed forever, they turned to present themselves in my room while the intense blue light shone again. I couldn't see but I sensed that they were in my room.

I heard a voice that identified with me in my mind and he said, "Hello, Augustin. Now we know everything about you. My name is Higer, I am the commander of the scientific expedition we are carrying out. We come from the star cluster called the Pleiades, the Seven Sisters in the English language; in the Japanese language, we are known within the Kanji script as Subaru and in Greek as the Seven Doves or the Cabrillas, the seven daughters of Atlas and Pleione, within their culture. The Aztecs called them Tianquiztli, which means 'meeting place' in the Nahuatl dialect and which is located within the constellation of Taurus in the star catalog of the Messier astronomer observer as M-45. Our star is located at a distance of approximately four hundred light years from Earth and its name is Alción, whose meaning is 'foundation'; is the most star of the star cluster, and its color is light blue due to its composition of particles that make it characteristic and of greater magnitude in brilliance to all the other sisters of her. The Pleiades constitute an open cluster of young stars and our planet is called Erra or Planet Erra, what a coincidence if you think about the similarity that exists with the name of the planet where you live! Slowly we will show you and give you wisdom according to your intellect."

Higer told me, "We have a mission that we want to share with you, of course, if you allow us." I felt such peace being with them that I told them, "Of course I accept!"

They asked me for all this telepathically, they never forced me, it was all my free will.

"We are ready to prepare you for your first mission, don't be afraid, everything will be fine, trust us," Higer told me.

"It's OK, go ahead!" I said.

Guatemala Earthquake

Suddenly I felt an impressive speed and a cold that I cannot explain myself, I don't remember if they took me physically or spiritually, everything is inside my subconscious. I was wondering how they could handle matter, time, and space, something I didn't understand. The cold and the speed indicated that we had arrived. Everything was dark. It was early in the morning, about half past three.

"I will be accompanying you all the time and I will be with you until finishing the missions entrusted to you. Now you are part of our group like other people we have assigned to other missions," Higer told me.

They left me on a street lonely and I only heard the barking of the dogs. Commander Higer, the alien, was with me and said, "Walk in that direction," and so I did.

I saw houses that were dimly lit by the light from the post, suddenly the Earth began to shake with great force, an earthquake shook the houses, and everything was thundering very strongly. A great despair took possession of me and my survival instinct made me run somewhere. I tried to hide in a church, but to my surprise when I entered the church it was dimly lit by candlelight; instinctively I turned towards the ceiling and saw the dome swaying; the chandelier was swaying back and forth. Suddenly the dome collapsed and fell. In the middle of the pews, the candles that were on the altars fell to the ground. I said to myself, all scared, "My God, I have to get out of here!" My despair was capitalized. I don't know how, but I almost flew out of the church, not running. It was all like a nightmare that I couldn't wake up.

I managed to get out and I was shocked when I saw people screaming, fire, and explosions everywhere. The lightning in the sky, the dogs howling, dead people, and others crying and running... everything was chaos, the land was so cracked that it opened up the streets.

Suddenly Higer grabbed me and said, "Let's go, it's enough with what you've seen!"

It was possible to imagine the relief I felt when we moved away from that place; everything was destroyed. Higer told me that place was called La Antigua, in Guatemala, and that he wanted me to give a message to warn the people to prepare for what was going to happen. Hearing this I felt again the vertigo of speed and that cold, suddenly I felt as if my feet had been pulled, just like in a dream, and woke up abruptly jumping from my bed. My body was completely bathed in sweat, I turned on the light that was in my bedroom and I thanked God that I was in my room safe and sound. I got ready to change the sheets because they were wet with perspiration. I went to the kitchen to have a drink of water and tried to sleep, I don't know if it was from shock but I fell into a very deep sleep.

The next morning I got ready to go to the minimarket. My sister Silvia was already waiting for me.

"You're a little late, you're always so punctual," she told me.

"If I told you what was happening to me, you wouldn't believe me," I answered.

That's how the morning passed and in the afternoon I remembered a client who worked at the time for the newspaper El Universal, I went to his house and he kindly received me. I told him I had some news that might interest him to see if he would write an article in the newspaper column, he said yes, and I invited him for coffee. With great caution, I told him about my contact with intelligent beings from another system and saw the look of surprise on his face. He politely listened to my story and at the end; he asked me,

"Is this an article based on a science fiction book?"

"Of course not!" I answered. What I am telling you is the truth and it is what is going to happen in the not-too-distant future.

After having the conversation I took him home and thanked him for his time and his attention. We said goodbye, but I felt in my heart that when he got home he was going to laugh at what I had told him during our meeting.

Time passed, and in my desperation, I was looking for the article in the newspaper, but it was not there. The day came when the earthquake was to happen; after the earthquake, I was passing the newsstand early in the day and El Universal and Excelsior gave the news of the earthquake that had occurred in Guatemala on the front page. The earthquake had an intensity of 7.5 degrees on the Richter scale, it had been recorded at 03:33 in the morning and had lasted 49 seconds; the earthquake had killed over 23,000 people and left a big destruction in its wake. What impressed me the most was seeing in the newspaper a photo of one of the damaged houses, that had been the last vision I had had before my teacher took me back.

Sometime later, I read an article in the newspaper that said that the cathedral of the city of La Antigua had been the one that had suffered more damage. Apparently, that had been the place where I had found myself. I turned pale, what Higer had told me had come true. The lady at the newsstand told me,

"Young man, are you feeling alright? You are very pale."

"Thanks, I'm fine, the thing is that the earthquake affected me too much," I replied.

I tried to discuss the phenomenon with her, but I remained silent; I thought, "If I tell her what happened with the extraterrestrial beings, she would make fun of me." I went back to my business, my head reeling from the impression I received when I was present. The fulfillment of said event shook me and put me in a situation of retraining about future visions or premonitions. Gradually my mind changed, every time someone greeted me I could see through them what they were like without the need to ask them. I was progressively changing from being a person happy and joyful to becoming a person isolated from others, thinking deep into the future and what God had prepared for us. I asked myself questions about what they had done to my Achilles heels and I needed to know if that was related to my way of thinking and seeing the past and the future, and with the voices I heard in my mind.

Deep feelings and visions awoke in me that I had never imagined.

When I paused, my friend Kyile told me, "

I'm very impressed. I have heard of isolated cases, but in general, they believe that these people are out of touch with reality, or are CRAZY."

"Here you are seeing my case," I replied. "They think I'm crazy, or that I smoke marijuana."

"It's very late! It's time to go home," he told me suddenly.

"Thanks for listening to me, Kyile."

"Don't worry, I believe you and I hope we continue talking," he told me.

From that conversation, Kyile was getting deeply interested in my personal experiences with my friends the aliens.

After the earthquake passed, my teacher Higer did not ask me why the article had not been written in the newspaper; I suppose that they knew the answer: who would have believed me?

One night when they took me, I was able to see them physically. My teacher Higer is approximately 5 feet tall, he has no hair, his eyes are oval and large, his skin is smooth and soft, light brown in color; his head is a little more bulging, a sign of great intelligence. They are physically similar to us but have noses and small mouths. His uniforms are metallic navy blue, but very tight to the body, and have black leather boots. The space suit has microfibers that keep their bodies at the temperature that they require when they are in other planetary systems since it allows them to reject any pathogenic bacteria that could cause an illness. It is also heat resistant at very cold temperatures, as my teacher Higer told me, it has the ability to repel an attack of a laser beam weapon or any type of weapon, of course, speaking of a melee attack.

Navigators or aliens who drive or operate the UFO were slightly smaller beings and of different physiognomy. His skin color was light brown, with oval eyes, a small nose, and a larger brain, a sign of prominent intelligence. According to my perception, its shape had very polite manners that radiated a peace that made me feel harmony and ecstasy I had never perceived in my life.

My teacher Higer sensed what I was thinking and told me, "Within our star cluster, in the Pleiades, there is a large number of beings highly intelligent that come from other galaxies and that have been with us exchanging and sharing biogenetic information that has allowed them to develop intellectually. We are talking about alien DNA, which is more advanced, than on Earth. You still have no idea. Our mission, in part, is to exchange with your biogenetic experiments that allow us to have new leaders on planet Earth who lead humanity towards a cosmic consciousness that allows them to develop in the near future. That was the Pleiadeans are taking care of human beings because you are our seeds of a Pleiadean culture, and planet Earth is currently facing collapse that will definitely lead the human race to its self-destruction, as it has happened on other planets due to mismanagement and the government. This is very obvious that planet Earth belongs to a reptilian government. That's why they are enslaving human beings, leaving them in a vicious circle where both education and the expression of belief are manipulated by personal ambitions and not according to the teaching of our messiah Jesus Christ. That is why God, within his infinite wisdom, has a renewal plan that will begin gradually to be carried out when the year 2012 begins.

We, the Pleiadians, cannot intervene in the formation and evolution of this."

I was highly surprised because when my teacher Higer referred to our Lord Jesus Christ, I understood that they were indoctrinated like us here on Earth to be part of an experiment. Scientists did not scare me—how and in what way they carried it out put me in a situation of suspense and nervousness because I still did not really know what they had done to my Achilles heels.

The next day I met Kyile again and he told me, "I want to ask you to tell me what is next."

"Now I'm buying lunch," I replied.

When it was time for lunch I continued telling him about my experience.

I told Kyile I could not resist asking them what they had really done to me, and when they came to visit me. I asked my teacher Higer what was done on my Achilles heels. He told me that they did a small surgery on me. The surgery was to insert some microchips to be able to have information about the composition of my genes, blood type, and everything; it would allow them to know if I was being affected or not being affected by performing numerous exams. It was to keep me healthy. and that every time I went out with them they would not affect my body the changes of my atmosphere and their presence, since they had a high rate of radiation within their electromagnetic fields and you could experience severe headaches, aneurysms, or blood clots.

"That is why we are doing extensive examinations and analyses: we must protect you and give you what you need to be able to stay physically and mentally strong. We are blocking your mind to prevent you from having trauma; as other people we have contacted are very sensitive or too nervous. You will notice that there will be situations or events that you will not be able to remember, but we will try to leave you with an open mind so you can remember the most important things and bear witness to our presence here on planet Earth and will be able to relay our messages. We need to put you in a physical and emotional environment to be able to continue with our present and future missions," Higer told me; and he added, "You cannot imagine what awaits you, for you it will be the first and great adventure in your life. Few beings of Earth are chosen like you to give a message to humanity. Microchips are part of the information we are receiving about your functioning organism and allow us to locate you and help you in case of a cardiac arrest, or a strong impression due to something unexpected, etc.

It was enough for me to know that I was being protected, but something inside of my being was gradually changing. I began to have visions and very wonderful dreams, a spiritual peace in which my mind opened to other dimensions that I could never have imagined. I understood that it is ridiculous to think that we are alone in the universe. One night—it was the Day of the Dead—I was able to verify it. My friends invited me to a party near a hill called La Tortuga, which is close to the highway. There, in that part, you can see the Valley of Mexico and the high influx of vehicles that circulate entering and leaving the Federal District. I went out to smoke a cigarette and suddenly I saw a UFO very bright white light in the shape of a sphere, quite large, in which you could see so many circular windows that let white light out.

I said to myself "Wow, how wonderful!"

It was easy for me to go to my car and make high-beam and low-beam changes to draw his attention, and when I did the UFO changed position from one hill to another in a second. I was amazed. It slowly moved north of the city until I lost sight of it.

My friend Jorge asked me why I wasn't at the party and I said that I had gone out to smoke a cigarette and that he would not believe what I had seen.

"What happened?" he told me.

"I saw a UFO!"

"Why didn't you call me?!"

Everything happened so fast that I was amazed watching it until he disappeared from my sight. I did not dare to tell him what had happened to me with my encounter with the third type because I did not know how he would take it or if his comments would be rude and offensive or if he would just laugh at me.

That same year a medium earthquake shook Mexico City. It was night, we were all asleep, suddenly the house moved from one side to the other and the construction structures thundered loudly. Instinctively, I jumped out of bed and went out to the garden. I saw the sky, it was red and flashing; that night I heard something unique and wonderful, as if a god or angels riding on his horses crossed the sky, and as the horses galloped, the tremor grew stronger. Suddenly I heard the sound of a trumpet, and when it stopped playing, the tremor slowly disappeared along with the riders on their steeds. Everything I saw and heard was kept in my heart since I did not dare to comment on it because they could say that I was losing my mind or that I was going crazy.

I went back to my bed to sleep. My parents were nervous and commented on what had happened. That night Higer did not show up and the next day I went back to my work routine. Several days passed without me knowing anything about my teacher and his companions, but one night they gave me a wonderful gift, it was a very pleasant surprise. The intense blue light was present in my bedroom and I noticed that this time it was more powerful, a very special aroma was present inside the room; it was incense or perfume that I had never smelled or experienced. Higer was accompanied by a very tall being whose look I remembered, he was very friendly. I felt a deep affection towards him. He told me his name but now I cannot remember it I had been impressed by the wonderful way he radiated peace, love, and that exquisite perfume that made me lose myself in the ecstasy of tranquility.

Then they asked me if I was ready and I said yes, "Always!" I felt the vertigo of speed; upon arrival, they showed me a very tall building and they took me out of their ship. I felt how they held me and the speed was present until I reached the top of the building. This time it was the wonderful extraterrestrial of impressive stature, he asked me,

"What do your eyes see?" "I know I'm in a building that's quite tall," I told him. I can see the white clouds of the sky and a blue that my eyes had never seen, this very special color.

Suddenly I saw some quite large herons and their plumage so white shimmering in the sun.

"What do you see, flying through the clouds?" he asked.

"I see some herons with beautiful and majestic plumage," I told him. They are flying so high that they touch the clouds.

"That's what you're seeing with your human eyes, but now I, as your new teacher, will make you see with spiritual eyes.

And as if a blindfold had fallen from my eyes, I was amazed to see how the herons were transfigured into angels of God. I felt a lump in my throat and I looked at my new spiritual teacher, who had told me, "

We will leave you here so you can enjoy what your spiritual eye is showing you."

Like a naughty child, they left me alone on the heights, I approached the edge of the top of the building and opened my arms as a sign that I wanted to touch them. I felt such an immense peace that I was crying and my eyes filled with tears and with great desire, I wanted to touch Angels. A heron with impressive plumage approached me and slowly began to lower and open its majestic wings until I hugged it. I was deeply moved. Suddenly it transformed into an angel of great stature, dressed in white, his belt was gold that shone like the sun, his blond hair radiated light, and his aroma enraptured me. I don't know how much time passed I wanted that wonderful moment to never end. I don't know how much I cried, I felt how the angel of God took me in his arms and I, like a child, fell asleep.

The next morning, when I woke up, my eyes were red from crying. My cheeks were cold with tears; I tried to remember everything that happened. I would have wanted to never wake up and go back to that wonderful place, but I had to go back to my usual routine. My brothers and my parents noticed my change but they thought it was the stress of work. Actually, I couldn't compare my special experiences. I couldn't compare them with each other, definitely not. I kept everything in my heart and in my thoughts for not being able to share it with someone; perhaps they would not have understood me and I would not have liked them making fun of my feelings. It matured little by little, but mainly spiritually. Of course, not everything in life is honey, I had problems like any human being and sometimes I collided emotionally.

I had a girlfriend, but we never formalized a relationship with marriage plans. It made me sad because sometimes I didn't have time to see her; she was a cheerful and very pretty girl, but unfortunately, I rarely got to be with her. One afternoon when I was at the business I began to think about her, unexpectedly I was visualizing a place that I was near the business, suddenly I saw her taking the arm of a boy and they were very happy and talked. I felt jealous and anxious; I said to my sister, "Please take care of the business, I'll be back in a few minutes."

I went quickly to that place where I had visualized them and suddenly I felt my blood run cold: there they were both kissing and hugging. When I approached them I complained, but she replied to me very upset

I lowered my head as a sign of respect and said,

"Excuse me, you're right, I'm sorry, I shouldn't have come to interrupt you," and sad, with tears on my cheeks, I turned around and went back to business.

My sister asked me what was wrong, I held back the urge to cry and told my sister it was nothing to worry about, that my girlfriend and I had just broken off our engagement. That night I went to a bar where they played romantic music and I was ready to get drunk.

I will never forget when the business owner approached me and he told me, "Hey boy, you're sad and hurt!"

"Yes, I broke up with my girlfriend. Well, rather, she's finished with me."

He looked at me tenderly, like a friend who respects pain, and he told me to have a drink on the house and asked his musicians on the side of the bar to play the "Baby Come Back" song. When they began to play, my tears began to roll down my cheeks. That night I don't remember how I got home or how much I drank.

My teacher Higer, on that occasion, did not approach me for my drunkenness, then one night he gave me an experience that I will never forget. It was already quite late and, due to my tiredness, I quickly fell into a deep sleep. As you know, sometimes we dream that we are in business or remembering things that happen to us. Suddenly I heard a voice saying to me, "Hey, turn around!"

My dream changed and I saw a small being about the size of a child but human in appearance, whose face, unlike ours, radiated much light. Smiling a lot, he told me telepathically, "Would you like to fly?"

I looked at him and asked, "How?"

"Don't worry, take my hand," he told me.

So I did it. I remember that I was surrounded by very beautiful houses and there was a sunset of white clouds and a very sunny day with the sky a wonderful blue, like the one I had seen in my vision of the angels of God. Suddenly I felt a cool breeze and we started to fly. He looked at me with a big smile as if wondering whether I was enjoying it, and I nodded my head approvingly. Suddenly, as though we had entered another dimension, I was seeing places very different from those seen here on our planet: an ocean of gentle crystal green waves, with white sand beaches; the formation of the rocks was a little different. There were so many very precious places.

I do not know how long we were in that paradise. In a moment he told me it was time to go back. I was so satisfied I did not object. Upon returning I began to see those pretty houses and I sighed so hard that I felt myself let go of the hand of my new friend, I was falling slowly, and I saw that I was getting dangerously close to the high-tension cables of an electric power tower. Desperately I tried to avoid them so as not to be electrocuted. He looked for me without being able to see me, until suddenly I touched the cables and the alarm of my alarm clock made me jump with fright. I got up abruptly and sat on the edge of my bed. I said to myself, "Thank you, my God, I didn't get electrocuted, it was just a dream!"

I returned to my daily routine but with a smile on my lips, my regular customers of the business would ask me why I was so happy, to which I replied, "I feel as if I were flying."I quietly enjoyed the wonderful experiences that my Pleiadian teachers gave me. It was true that my job enslaved me, but my extraterrestrial brothers spiritually rewarded my hard work. I remember that one Sunday, being alone at home after have dinner, I got ready to listen to music accompanied by a glass of white wine. That was the saddest afternoon of my life. without asking permission or help from Higer, my teacher, I used my senses to be able to see into the future and, as time progressed, they presented images of my parents and I saw how in the not-too-distant future my father was going to die, and then there were other unpleasant events that were predestined to change my life. That night I cried lovingly, I would have liked not to know how to use my senses to be able to see into the future; Higer's presence took away my sorrow and he said,

"I wish I could tell you what you saw now, but I left it to your free will. There is no human power that can change destiny, what is already written is in the hands of God.

"It's painful to lose a loved one," I told him, "but I feel like you're telling me in an insensitive way. Tell me how you see life. Have you scientifically developed a way of prolonging life forever?

Smiling at me in a very special way, he told me,

"We Pleiadians figured out how we can prolong life, but not forever, that's up to God. The time will come to show you the love of God and his purposes for you and humanity, for now, rest, sleep, and do not torment yourself."

I felt how he put his hands on my head and I fell into such a deep dream. That next morning I opened the minimarket late. My sister told me that it was already becoming a habit. I did not really feel tired, I completely forgot my visions and, putting on a smiling face, I told my sister,

"I had a dream but it wasn't flattering." Give thanks to God because you have health and this business that puts food on the table for you," and my sister smiled.

Of course, my sister did not openly know about the encounter with extraterrestrial beings.

It was a Monday and it was time to get off work. Kyile, my terminal manager, called me on my cell phone and said, "I'll see you at seven at the same restaurant; I came and he asked me,

"Is there anything interesting you can tell me?"

"Can you really believe what's happening to me?" I said.

"I believe you, everything is possible," he affirmed while smiling at me.

Moreover, I kept narrating.

Three years of great events and premonitions passed, for example, Higer told me that the Popocatepetl volcano in Mexico was going to erupt, but they told me they had a mission to be able to calm it, it was too dangerous since that volcano was higher in activity than the one from Krakatoa I'm talking about three times more powerful, can you imagine an explosion of three nuclear bombs? That is why the presence of UFOs was detected when the volcano began to erupt. A reporter from a Mexico City newspaper was able to take a photograph when the volcano began to have activity, they reported the appearance of the UFO that entered the volcano and in minutes it stopped erupting, which the public was informed in the newspaper that dealt with the event that occurred. The image that the journalist captured on camera of this is impressive.

Higer told me that they were diverting the volcanic magma to other places where there are sulfurous waters, for example in the state of Puebla. Volcanic activity worldwide is becoming more intense due to changes within the magnetism of the Earth by the changes caused by the loss of ozone in the atmosphere. This causes a disturbance to the globe and also affects all the other planets in our solar system, due to that the Sun is also in a phase of even more violent eruptions than on previous dates. Consequently, the Sun will gradually go from being a medium G-type star to being a red giant, which through the years will increase. The heat will affect every planet. The heliosphere of the Sun has a magnetic field that is taking us to a new level of energy and that increase will change the nature of every human being.

I was also remembering that in all my dreams there appeared a jet with passengers and there was a hill that had a very big sign that said "PRI." Suddenly the jet was flying too close to the hill and crashed where the sign of that party was painted. Sometime after the official party of the PRI, after 74 years, his reign of corruption and murder ended. The strongest politician match collapsed causing a political uproar in the country of Mexico."Also in my dreams, I heard the cry of a child, It gave me a great feeling and I woke up at night sighing and crying, I couldn't take it anymore and I asked Higer when he was present, "Why every night in my dreams do I hear the cry of a baby? Tell me why, Higer."

"The cry you hear in your dreams is your baby," he said. "You've had it with a woman from our planet. He is approximately three years in Earth age."

"Is what you're telling me true?" How could it happen?"

I asked him.

"One night you were asleep and we took you to our ship, we already had it prepared beforehand," Higer told me. "We are giving life to beings of our planetary system with yours because the planet Earth, in the not-too-distant future, will suffer earthquakes as big as Atlantis Mu and Lemuria. We are looking for the best form of adaptation of the human being with our race within our cluster of the Pleiades and seeing that the atmosphere inside our planets is ideal for the future coexistence of the human being and our people. It is true that you do not remember many things because we block your mind so as not to cause you stress or trauma, but we asked you if you wanted to have sexual relations with one of our women, and you obviously said yes. You even jumped for joy."

I couldn't contain my laughter and said, "Why can't I remember all those things that happened to me?"

"Perhaps you wouldn't have liked her physically, but when we put a special cream on you to make you sexually aroused, you put no objection. But," said my teacher, and smiled in a special way, "I saw your expression of satisfaction when we took you back home."

I scratched my head trying to think of why I couldn't remember what had happened that night, not because of morbidity but of knowing what my extraterrestrial companion was like physically, and I wanted to know if someday I could see the baby boy. Higer told me that when the time was right I could see him and hug him. Then my question was when the Earth would collapse like Atlantis. I personally asked myself, "Did Atlantis Mu and Lemuria really exist?"; Higer told me that I would know everything at my time in a future time.

I was still wondering about the baby, but Higer told me that at that moment they had him preparing himself as a great scientist. I was amazed, but can you imagine if I discussed it with people? They would treat me as mentally ill and deranged. Higer replied that for them it was normal for beings from other planets to have an approach, that there was nothing abnormal, and that everything was part of a life cycle. Obviously, you on Earth can't even have a clue about it. Every day I understood that if God had formed such a large universe, it was not for only human beings to inhabit it, because that was ridiculous, stupid, and selfish. One night my teacher gave me a thorn projection due to my insistence about the Pleiadean girl, everything started when I was taken to the mothership, we were orbiting around the earth, and the Pleiadeans' biogenetic doctors prepared me in the lab, I was in a kind of hospital bed lying down preparing my body with special creams in my abdomen, the biogenetic scientist told me that the special lotion is to help me to get sexually excited, when I was ready they took me to another compartment or room. When he touched the wall of the ship with his hand, a compartment opened, it was a bedroom and the biogenetic doctor took the clothes out of my body and left me naked, suddenly the Pleiadean girl approached me and extended her hand so that I could take hers. She was naked and I could see her beautiful body, she had blonde hair and expressive blue-gray colored eyes. In the private bedroom, she invited me to lie down on the bed and we started having sex, the light in the room was illuminated, and after having sex she was talking to me telepathically and told me, "Hold my hand."

She was touching the wall of the UFO and opened a special oval window changing color from metal to a transparent (clear) window showing what was outside. We were orbiting between the moon and the Earth. It was a beautiful view, nothing like I have ever seen in my life, with her mind she was asking me if liked the view. I told her it was a wonderful view, we were completely naked, and we were hugging. I was holding her waist, we enjoyed the view. After we started dressing up, she kissed me and said goodbye! Crying with tears in my eyes for those moments of happiness, she opened the door after touching it with her hand and disappeared. The scientist escorted me to the lab and took me to the shower and after drying off my body, a special air to sterilize my body came out. That was what the biogenetic doctor told me, after they took me back home, when I woke up I couldn't remember anything.I continued narrating my story to Kyile.

After selling the business in Mexico, I dedicated myself to another activity. I was a tourist carrier. I was still alone, had no girlfriend, and had no commitment. When visiting the ruins of Chichen Itzá, in Mérida, Yucatán; in Monte Albán and Teotihuacán, the truth is that I stayed amazed, I asked myself a thousand questions about who had been the authors and how they had been able to build such immense pyramids of marvelous architecture. How was it possible that, having such devastating storms, they would have had a drainage system that not even our modern cities currently have?

After having made several trips to different parts of the Republic of Mexico, day by day I was more amazed by the pyramids, our history, and the museums. I arrived home after long trips through the interior of the republic and prepared to take a few days off. I don't know why but I sensed that my life was already predestined to something, to events; little by little everything was appearing to me according to a plan and everything seemed to indicate that it was so because the night Higer arrived he told the master chief navigation of the UFO to take coordinates towards Machu Picchu. The blue light strongly illuminated the bedroom of my room and we left at dawn towards that place.

My teacher Higer told me, "I know that you were highly impressed with what you saw on the trips to the pyramids, so now we are going to show you who its architects were." The UFO this time supposedly moving at a medium speed; the navigation commander bosun moved something inside the UFO panel and changed the cab interior from sky blue to metallic orange to silver. Suddenly a window was seen opening inside the cabin and showing me the face of the Earth, we were flying over the Pacific Ocean it started to change. the hour, we were approaching the Earth and from the heights, a figure could be observed, it was an extraterrestrial being that friendly greeted me with his hand, we were in Nazca. As Higer showed me, we saw different figures, but I was too surprised by the figure of the alien who was waving, a figure too large to be seen on Earth.

I paused to say to Kyile, "This is going to be one of the experiences that is going to surprise you, it is about who were the builders of the pyramids and why the Incas and Mayans were advanced in knowledge astronomical and architectural." Then I continued with this story.

Higer began to tell me more about the origin of the pyramid builders around the world and told me that they, the Pleiadians, were the teachers of the Mayans. Incas, Aztecs, Egyptians, and Greeks; their community was made up of all the inhabitants of their stars, seven stars in particular, formed by their respective planets. That divine mandate of their great teacher, they had decided to come to Earth and build the pyramids and the names of those stars were: Alción, Maia, Celeno, Electra, Esterope, Tay geta, and Merope. According to mythology, all those stars were daughters of Atlas and Pleione. Also was present the extraterrestrial from Venus, Sirio, Orion, and other stars.

He told me that his stellar community in the Pleiades was quite large and that each community of said stars had taken charge to carry out the construction of the pyramids. Higer told me that He was going to show me why they had decided to carry out these pyramidal constructions and he explained it to me by saying that, due to the fields magnets of the Earth, this type of construction stores an energy electromagnetic field, together with the Sun, allows it to serve as gigantic radio telescopes that can be used as communication routes within her star cluster. That's why the pyramids are with those stars, mainly Alcyone, which is the brightest in magnitude and that, together with the Sun and the Earth, marks the center of its cluster and the center of the Milky Way.

My teacher made it clear to me that, certainly, as the years went by and by shifting the Earth's axis, some electromagnetic variation had been lost. Regarding the terrestrial position, the reason for building astronomical observatories consisted in giving knowledge to the Mayans, Incas, and Aztecs about the movement of the stars and dates so that they "could have exact knowledge of our position, of our cluster and of more constellations." Certainly, the pyramids were built for the equinoxes and solstices, and resulted in the knowledge of implementing the harvest dates, among other things; Mayan and Aztec calendars were the most advanced to date, unequaled in accuracy and prediction, as they mark the completions of the ages on this planet, impossible for humans being to have built them.

Higer went on to teach me that Quetzalcoatl was recognized by the Aztecs as a God, but that they, the Pleiadians, called him Master of Light, who comes from the high hierarchies through a divine plan, and that he was sent to give light and wisdom to the world.

I paused briefly and told Kyile that Higer had given more information but that there was little that I could remember due to my work and my tiredness.

"I know that I have more valuable information within my subconscious but you know that hypnotherapy is expensive and unfortunately I do not have enough capital to be able to do regressive therapies. In addition, until now no one has been interested in my personal experience, everything has remained in the dark, however, let me tell you that it has been a wonderful experience for me personally because they are providing me with information hereto unknown to humanity." Indeed, Higer had told me that after his departure, upon completion of the construction of the pyramids, many nobles had decided to go with the Pleiadians to their star cluster. Because the great Mayan, Inca, and Aztec nobles saw that time passed and knew nothing of their gods and teachers, all the splendor of their cultures began to succumb to internal political and social problems. No government can be sustained without the guidance of God and it is true that much information was lost since the arrival of the Spaniards all the codices were destroyed, their cities were looted and the temples burned. Thus they left adrift great knowledge and wisdom. It is true that few codices were saved but, unfortunately, they are in other countries and if there are some others, they were never deciphered or made public; How sad.

When we arrived at Machu Picchu I remember that they left me at the main entrance. He remembered the stones and how the pyramids were built, they were a wonderful sight. I saw the indigenous people of that place with their typical clothes but in them, I could perceive that his look was sad and his face aged, I don't know why, but that's how I saw it. As he climbed towards the pyramids I saw the looks of the old men and women, they looked tired. I reached a certain altitude and I could see an area where there was an avenue that reached an esplanade, it was pressing to see that place due to the immense altitude.

After walking for a while, my teacher Higer told me, "Come on, I'm going to show you another area that was originally one of the most important ceremonial centers. They took me to a place that was about 60 miles away; the name I do not remember, but what I do remember was the following:

Higer dropped me off at the entrance to a pyramid that had been in back then a very important ceremonial center took place, according to what he had described to me. I walked inside the pyramid but I saw another exit and suddenly I found something that looked like a grotto or cavern, although it was brightly lit. I remember I had a small stream of crystal clear water, I listened to the murmur of the running water, and I was fascinated; the water was up to my ankles and it guided me into the cavern.

Suddenly I heard a voice who, in an impressive but subtle tone, told me, "Take off your shoes, you are stepping on a sacred place."

I obeyed immediately and, making a bowing with a bow of the head, I heard again the voice telling me to kneel down. I did so. When I raised my face little by little, I saw that in the middle of the cool river of crystalline water there was a triangular quartz that illuminated the grotto was something wonderful, it was a stone with three sides and it was about five feet. high, it was very resplendent. Apparently, it was there where God had manifested himself in a remote time to the ancient Incas. In my vision, I heard in the distance the music of the Incas with quena flutes, like a murmur that was confused with the running of the stream water. So my vision was slowly fading with that wonderful music. That morning I woke up with very encouragement to start my workday, I had many visions and prophetic dreams, and I commented on them enthusiastically but all the people ignored me, he was used to it, but all that fed me spiritually.

Time went by, several tourists encouraged me to go to the United States. I got my visa and got ready to visit the city of Los Angeles, CA. It was 1985, and I was still single, I decided to stay and when I was already working; I began to think of who my future wife would be, I slept in an equipped van. The friends I saw myself with invited me to drink and I liked to drink, at one of those parties I drank too much and the next morning, when I was working in the warehouse in the city of South Gate, I told my supervisor, "I went to a party and drank too much." I don't feel good, I need to go lie down.

My supervisor told me, "You have a fever. You'd better go see the doctor."

I don't know how, but I remember driving to the General Hospital and I arrived at the emergency room. They quickly transferred me to a stretcher and they administered serum to me, I lost consciousness until the next day I was able to recover my memory. My current wife, who at that time was my girlfriend, found out about me and went to visit me at the hospital. Time after she left and I was left alone, the fever did not subside and they put towels on my head with water and enough serum. Several doctors came to see me and I got the impression from their gestures that I was not doing good. They gave me a sleeping aide that made me sleep all afternoon. I don't know what time it was when I woke up, because the nurse moved me to change my I.V. and then she left.

That night Higer, my teacher, showed up and approached me for what I had done. I apologized and told him that I thought he had ended our close friendship. On the contrary, he told me,

"Now you are going to enter another stage of your life that will make you change your way of thinking forever. We are going to cause you to die physically to be able to show you the purpose of our mission here on the planet Earth."

"If I'm going to die, what's the purpose?" I asked, why? Obviously, I couldn't understand, I was under the effect of strong narcotics and serums; I immediately said to Higer, "Here I am, go ahead.

Suddenly I felt as if I had a cardiac arrest, I felt an immense peace, I began to float, and I saw myself in my bed.

"Come, go to where this tunnel is," my teacher told me.

I felt scared and he tried to reassure me, "Come in, don't be afraid."

In that tunnel I saw a dark round cave shape, there was no light, I felt an immense peace but at the same time terror. My teacher Higer told me to keep walking.

"Do you see that dim light beyond?

"Yes, I see it," I replied.

I no longer walked. I felt that I was running as the light became more intense. When the tunnel ended, the light was wonderful. Higer told me to come in, and to my surprise, I saw between the clouds a sky-blue vision of polished iron gates that were so big. Here it was great. Suddenly the bars of that wonderful place opened and I saw a bearded man wearing a white robe and very resplendent and in his hands he had some very large golden keys; he had a sweet and peaceful look; he invited me to come in.

I remember that Higer was not with me; I walked a bit and he told me to get naked because I was going to go into a crystal clear pool of water I walked towards that pond and there was a waterfall like a small waterfall, I submerged myself and felt such an immense peace that I did not want to have to get out of there. The bearded man told me to come out and he put a robe on me. Around him were two winged angels who assisted him, they were very tall, human in appearance but very blond, with long hair, and their white robes radiated a lot of light; They had a sweet and peaceful look that gave me a security of peace that I never felt in my life.

The bearded man told me to follow him and that he was going to show me what was allowed. We walked through a beautiful garden and we arrived where I could see a very large building that seemed more like a medieval castle, although it had too many windows. Arriving At the entrance, I noticed that it had white marble steps that shimmered in the sunlight. The entrance was very wide, it had a very pretty door that was wide open. In that wide corridor, I saw some beds that reminded me of a hospital, they were clean and shiny, but no one was sick.

The man asked me, "What do you see?"

"I see many beds but I don't see any sick or hurt person," he replied. "They are empty because there are no people here ill or recovering from an illness," the bearded man said.

The truth is that perhaps I could not understand correctly why obviously there are no sick bodies. There are spirits that need to recover when one dies, that's what I could understand according to my understanding, because although I was physically dead, spiritually I was healthy and without any pain. The bearded man said that was all he was allowed to show me and that it was time to return.

We walked through that beautiful garden, there were little birds and peace accompanied us back to where that huge iron gate was, then he took out his keys and unlocked it.

"It's time to go back," he told me.

"No, I don't want to go back," I said, and I hugged him crying.

"You have to go back, it's not your time yet," he told me while he smiled tenderly at me and hugged me.

My guide and spiritual teacher approached and took me by the shoulder. He told me that we had to go back, that what I had seen was enough for the moment. This time I felt Higer very upset. He did not have words to ask me, I looked back and could see that the bearded man closed the huge gate and disappeared as if he vanished into the clouds. I saw the hole, I went in and I felt as if it were pulling me; I had visions of my childhood and my present age as if I had been watching a movie screen all my life.

When I woke up I got out of bed, but the IV needles hurt my veins and I ended up covered in blood. A doctor came in and told me not to worry, that he was going to take care of me He did it quickly and smiling and said goodbye to me. I felt like I was in the clouds, I don't know if it was because of the antibiotics or the impression, I was very dizzy. Then a nurse came and she asked me who had changed me, I replied that a doctor did and she looked puzzled. I described the doctor: blond-haired, young, and tall; I told her that when he had finished changing me he had told me not to worry, that I would be fine. The nurse said that there was no doctor on duty at the time and that the doctor would arrive in ten minutes. She was checking me out and she told me that the young doctor I had men tioned had given me an excellent change of IV strips, but she kept wondering who would that doctor be.

Now that time has passed and I have remembered all my experiences, the only thing I can tell you, Kyile, is that he was an angel who saw to it that I returned to Earth safely.

"I agree," he told me, "but honestly I never have been able to see or speak with an angel. I am extremely impressed with your personal experiences. I left the hospital discharged and fully recovered. God had healed me but still did not understand that drinking caused me damage, I stopped drinking for a period and then returned the same, I liked alcohol.

Time passed and the day came when my wife and I united our lives in marriage. After a year and a half, my wife became pregnant, but during her visit to the doctor, far from receiving good prognoses, we found out that something was wrong with the baby, it was developing in the fallopian tubes, which would cause her death. The doctor ruled that my wife had to undergo an emergency operation the next morning to prevent complications. The news affected us deeply. My wife was inconsolable, I didn't know what to say to her, she was shattered.

My wife was hospitalized that night to be operated on early the next day. When I got home I cried like never before, that's when Higer came and told me, "Don't worry."

"How can you tell me such a thing? We are losing our baby," I told him.

"Do you have faith?" he asked me.

"Yes," I affirmed, "with that great faith that God has shown me… But do you know that the baby is going to be lost?"

"For God, there is nothing impossible," he replied. "He is the Creator of life throughout the universe and if this is happening, it is for his glory to be displayed in you and your wife, trust in God!"

Resigned by the events, that night at home I felt the loneliness of not seeing my wife with me and of not being able to contemplate the loss of our baby. I cried like never before, blaming God for what was happening to us, to go through that situation, and between his pyros and cries I fell asleep, but late at night my teacher Higer was present and gave me a kiss on the forehead, he told me that he had come to show me what God the Father wanted me to fulfill according to his purpose. Higer put his hands on my forehead and I fell into a deep sleep. Inside my vision, I remember that it had finished raining and the sky was dark; it was a cold morning, and in the distance, you could see the dark clouds contrasting with the light of the sun to start the end of a turbulent rain.

I remember that I was supposedly walking down a street that I was going uphill and I was holding my daughter in my left hand, she was little, she was starting to walk and we were going slowly. On the other side of the street, I saw a lot of crystal clear water flowing, but it was very turbulent. It was running too fast when suddenly the water increased the level of the current and became violent and snatched my daughter from my hands; Desperate, I tried to run down the street, but I saw that my daughter was carried away by the current. I screamed and cried because of the anguish of not being able to reach her. Suddenly a woman appeared with a white dress in the middle of the water, she took the arms of my daughter and smiled at me, she handed her to me. I saw that the water was running through her legs but didn't move her. I thanked him and continued my way home. I turned to see my daughter and she was smiling at me; her face was engraved in my mind and in my heart. I remember we left walking and we entered a house with red bricks and trees.

That morning I woke up sad and with a heavy heart. I was about to go to the hospital to see my wife. After the operation she was inconsolable over the loss of our baby, I didn't have the courage to tell her about the dream I had that night. The next day my wife was released from the hospital; It took several days for her to recover. Thus the months passed, we did not speak of the subject, the wound caused did not allow us to be able to accept it; however, in my heart, I kept the experience of the promise of the woman dressed in white who would one day return our daughter to us.

Now I know that this wonderful woman is the Mother of our Lord Jesus Christ and that sometime later she would return our daughter, which had been lost in the operation. I still remember the words of my teacher Higer: "Do not lose faith. she will be returned to you and the Glory of God will be displayed in you."

Sometime later our first daughter was born, Vanessa Osornio. I remember that dream of her, her features, and her smile, I see the same features in her as in the first baby.

Time continued to pass; Higer was no longer present constantly. He once told me that there was a concern very large by the community of Pleiadian scientists about the future of the Earth, first because of the earthquake so big which took place in Mexico City. It was in 1985 and on a Thursday, September 19; according to data provided by news agencies, it was a magnitude of 8.1 degrees on the Richter scale and lasted two minutes, which exceeded the intensity of the earthquake in 1957—on July 28—in the same city. It left thousands dead and left people destitute, living in the streets, out in the open. The official data provided by the agencies that investigated the death of the people exceeded the figure given by the government, which the press hid from the public, and the true statistics of mortality since the actual death toll was over 40,000 deceased.

I only remember, before coming to the United States, that in Mexico City I lived in an atmosphere of violence and hatred, the people were very aggressive, and there was no respect for others. After the earthquake, when I returned to see my brothers and my parents to see how they were, all the people looked different, the violence had subsided and everyone was trying to help each other. How God changes people: yesterday was violent and, time then calmed them. But even the poorest people were the most affected, they continued to sleep in the streets, experiencing cold and discomfort. I remember that my relatives told me that in the middle of the streets, it smelled like corpses fetus, which was an ugly scene and sad; streets, littered with rubble and destruction, it took months to return to calm, but the reconstruction of the city took longer. It seems unbelievable: we all saw earthquakes as phenomena of nature and we do not ask ourselves who their Creator is.

Not only did my mind grasp that who is behind nature is God, but my spirit also felt divine wrath because He is certainly just and merciful but be careful when we cause Him harm. God was trying to change my life by putting Higer as my spiritual master, but I, like every human being, still kept making my mistakes and kept getting drunk, which Higer didn't approve of. After my two daughters were born, María Eugenia and Yolanda, I changed a bit, it calmed me down for a while but then returned to the same despite the fact that in dreams and visions, I saw the Glory of God.

Time passed and events continued to happen in my life, which left a very deep impression on me. On a Sunday I went with my wife and my daughters to have breakfast; I went to the restaurant and parked the car. A man was walking with his approximately ten-year-old son; When I got out of my vehicle and moved forward a little, the young man approached me and hugged me. I felt an immense desire to cry because that creature had transmitted the Spirit of God to me. The father of the young man apologized to me and I told him no, please let him hug him. The boy suffered from Down syndrome; God was showing at that time that in those special people, he manifested his Spirit. I couldn't find words to explain all those wonderful situations in which my God opened my spirituality, we must not reject, but show our love. Gradually I accepted what my God wanted to show me and that was the duty to give love to others because they carry the purity of the soul.

I thought that was why Higer was gradually moving away from me because he showed me situations I didn't understand. Well, that was what I thought, but it was not until sometime later that my teacher returned to make an act of presence in my life.

When he introduced himself, he spoke to me in a very strong tone and said, "You are entering the culmination part of our engagement, you are no longer part of a scientific experiment, now you form part of the purpose of the Kingdom of God. Gradually we are showing His love and mercy. I have fulfilled my purpose as your teacher, but now you are going to become part of a purpose saint, that's why I ask you to stay away from everything that displeases God."

"I'm trying to change, but my problems distract me from all the good things that you show me," I told him, "and it seems that I can get out of that hole in which I am submerged."

"You are entering a stage in which they are going to show you stronger things, so you have to be prepared mentally and spiritually," Higer clarified. We'll be back to show you what God wants you to see and experience so that you can bear witness to what exists. Humans must know that what you are going to see is real and must learn that their race is being dragged down by the forces of evil spirits.

Some time passed; when Higer showed up, he told me that he was not afraid of what he was going to see and hear, because the angels of the Lord would accompany me and protect me. I replied that he did not fear, that we continued forward with the design. That night terrifying things appeared in my vision: I was in a dark and cold cavern, and I was chained with shackles on my wrists, so I was hanging unable to move; felt the presence of the angels who guarded me and who illuminated the cave where I was. Suddenly, devils and disgusting and horrible figures appeared, blaspheming and insulting the name of the Lord and they tried to hurt me, but when the angels of God illuminated the grotto with their swords, they stopped, saying, "For Why have they come to torture us ahead of time?

I was terrified of seeing those demons and horrible beings. I felt that I was going to die, I was in great anguish and despair. The presence of the angels of God with their swords that shone like fire prevented those horrible beings from approaching me. When one of the angels broke the chains that held me and the other angel of the Lord waved his sword menacingly against those disgusting beings who ran to the bottom of the cave, there were those creatures of the Lord They took me by the shoulders and took me out of that horrible place.

When I woke up the next morning, I had a heavy brain and everything was spinning. It took me time to recover.

We went to mass that Sunday and I was meditating on what had happened, I felt how God had given me spiritual strength and how that fire burned my insides; then I understood more deeply what it was that God, my Lord, wanted me to do, that's why I dared to witness in the churches, but as always happens, some believed and others did not.

I now understood my master's purpose and haste so that I would be instructed and receive the Spirit of God in my life, because that way I could give a message to humanity.

I remember when Higer told me that they hadn't had a government for thousands of years. When they decided to have God as a guide and teacher, God gave them the power of wisdom—like Solomon—and seeing that they were pleasing in his eyes, he allowed them the Pleiadians to reach a range of knowledge to be able to bring divine love to other communities. The Earth, being the dais of God, was great and resplendent in the time of King David and King Solomon, but after passing through other kings, the power of the people of Israel fell into sin and provoked the wrath of God. So God turned away from them. I dared to ask Higer if there were beings similar to us in other stars, to which he replied that of course and that in due time would be shown to all beings human that not only here on planet Earth is there life. That's why God, with his infinite wisdom, has given life to other beings of appearance different from ours and, being the Pleiadians part of a culture that he has come to be faithful to God, he has appointed them as the disciples of that great community that shows the glory of God and ridicules to scientists and humans who believe they are the only beings living in the universe. People who don't believe will already have their response time.

Everything was clearing up in my mind; in my understanding, the Pleiadians are disciples of our Lord Jesus Christ and God the Father, who was showing me his kingdom according to his design and not according to human criteria.

I remember very clearly one night I had a prophetic dream. My teacher was not present, but I felt the presence of an angel of God, who took me to the ocean and told me to put pay attention to what I saw because that would be a hurricane of great magnitude that would hit the Earth. "They will not consider it of greater importance—warned—but watch what is going to happen." Then I saw the hand of God going down to the ocean and how a finger of God dipped into the waters and suddenly began to form a whirlpool that gradually became a hurricane. The angel of the Lord told me that was all he had to show me, go and get ready to give them the news.

When I woke up I was very restless and in a bad mood. one and a thousand questions about who could listen to me or believe in my prophetic dream at lunchtime I called El Show de Cristina and They told me I had to talk to a producer, but the only thing I happened was that they put me in a voicemail, which never returned to me the call. I understood that they were too busy and the next day I sent them an e-mail that they never answered. Try to notify the media but nobody gave importance to the hurricane.

When I met Kyile, he told me, "Do you have something new to tell me?"

"Yes, Kyile," I answered very sadly. A hurricane of great is coming magnitude, but people do not believe it. I went to the media, but they paid me no attention.

Kyile just listened to me.

Sometime later the hurricane already had a name—Kathrina—and was moving dangerously over the coast of Florida, but gave a turn and went to hit the shores of New Orleans. People It was drinking and enjoying as if such a phenomenon was not going to be of great intensity, however, what a surprise they got when He left death and destruction in his wake, but everything happens by the will of God. According to what they said, there, in that place, people surrendered to prostitution and all those things that displease God, that place They called Little Sodom and Gomorrah. It took time for the city to return to calm. Many people actually believed that it had been the wrath of God, but others, as always, said that there has been a thing of nature.

I am currently seeing the changes that are taking place on our planet, clearly, it shows that there is a time when the prophecies will be fulfilled, to tell the truth since the time of Solomon and King David we have seen that in the Bible the prophets of God were ignored and put to death by people who never showed fear of God and who, on the contrary, was always haughty and challenger before his Creator. I wonder what became of those people. Certainly, the Bible speaks of such people who in later times will be proud and will challenge God, they will insult him and blaspheme. Currently, it is being seen that Satan is attracting more disciples to his congregation, dragging young people to perdition without knowing that the punishment for disobedience to God is eternal. Poor those people who do not know the terrible punishment that awaits them.

It is known that in New York they are buying abandoned churches to carry out satanic acts killing innocent children and offering them in sacrifice to Lucifer. Certainly, the power of evil is great, see in the Catholic churches how the diabolical forces are manifesting themselves, for example in the priests who are raping young people and girls. How is it possible that the Vatican does not try to do anything to stop these sexual predators that society calls pederasts? It is ridiculous and stupid that these unfortunate abusers have their names without the Vatican or the authorities doing anything to stop them. That's why God has great anger against them.

It was the year 2006 when I received a visit from Higer. He told me that the Pleiadians were on other missions at the bottom of the oceans because there was a very big concern: Due to the ozone loss, global warming was causing the oceans could have fractures, which covered the plate with volcanic magma and caused cracks that allowed gases to escape from the magma. If this happened, the planet Earth could face one of the greatest catastrophes since the ice age during which the dinosaurs were extinct. That is why the media had given the alert call in case of seeing sightings of UFOs or "USOS," acronyms in the English language that come from "Unidentified Underwater Objects" in the oceans. Effectively they were trying to prevent the Earth from leaking volcanic gases that are deadly for the planet since they could come into contact with the atmosphere and cause a chain reaction higher than several nuclear detonations.

The USOS are Pleiadian ships that have the technology to be able to control the faults in the tectonic plates at the bottom of the oceans. This is what my teacher informed me: He was going to take me to a place where the Earth would be devastated by a huge earthquake; the wrath of God was great. They left me in the San Francisco Bay, precisely over a train stop I could see the bench and the part where he covered the bench to protect himself from the sun, and could contemplate the famous Golden Gate Bridge, I could clearly hear the train bells. I saw a circular clock at the station that marked approximately half past twelve, it was sunny. Suddenly the Earth began to shake, I saw that the train was submerged in the waters from the sea, the buildings collapsed and so did everything around me. People screamed crying in despair, sinking us into the depths of the waters, which were clean and crystal clear.

I felt that I was short of breath and I was drowning, I made an attempt to get out but little by little I was dragged towards the depths. I felt myself passing out, but when I came to I screamed so loud that I woke up my wife, who asked me if I was well. I looked around and saw that she was in my bed, reacting I said sorry. That was one of the truest impressions I had since, I had no doubt that San Francisco would be the next city touched by divine wrath, when I didn't know, well that belonged only to God.

Several nights passed without hearing from Higer. time after it was done present and he asked me if he had paid attention to the vision of St. Francisco, because that city was destined to be punished. Their inhabitants had defied the Creator by making the place the capital of lesbians and gays. God formed man and woman so that they might have understanding, but not man with man and woman with woman. He told me that even if I gave the message they would not believe me, that it was a matter of time before God decided how to punish them That's my biggest concern right now. that if San Francisco were to be hit by the most devastating earthquake in history, it would not only be that city but also Los Angeles. and part of Mexico, since the San Andreas fault goes beyond the US territory.

God has had mercy for that reason the prophecy has not been fulfilled.

For this reason, I decided to write this book. I am not speaking on behalf of any religion nor am I judging the way that people are leading their lives. Yes, it is true that God is manifesting in my existence and it does not mean that I walk on tiptoes with a harp in the sky, of course not, I also have my tail that drags me and in no time am I saying that I am a prophet of the Lord. Why was I chosen to give these messages? I can only answer that both you and I or those other people are touched by a divine purpose but do not think that I am a soul of God, I have my mistakes and failures as any human being and the truth is that if I did not decide to write this before, was for being mocked by so many people.

Now everything is a purpose of God and if He wants it to be his messenger, so it will be, believe me, or not. In due time you will be witnesses when greater events come. As my Lord Jesus Christ said, "Whoever has ears let him hear, and whoever wants to see he see." I do not represent any congregation of any religion or sect, everything is according to my free will. whoever wants to believe in the message he creates. I do everything for love, to serve our Divine Master Jesus Christ. I'm still a human being who drags the crap of me, but with a difference: God touched me and the truth is that little by little He is changing my life.

I try to push myself to be better, but I keep seeing myself here on Earth; I drag my problems, the envy of others, selfishness, and indifference of others, that is part of the planet Earth. What I knew through extraterrestrial beings is light and love, while here on Earth the governments are very busy destroying the human being and chaining them to ignorance, they do a cover-up for his personal purposes alluding to the fact that beings aliens do not exist, that there is no life on other planets. If that is so why then are they spending too many millions of dollars in searching for intelligent life on other planets that might exist and harboring humans in the future?

My teacher's response was immediate and he told me like this: "Da a message to the inhabitants of the Earth. If we, the Pleiadians, along with other civilizations of extraterrestrial beings, as well as they call us, do not make ourselves present on Earth, it is for different reasons. In the first place, for example, when other civilizations of extraterrestrial beings arrive, they see a world where there are wars, perdition, envy, selfishness, and theft; nations fighting to dominate the weak, corrupt, and murderous presidents who build walls to divide countries by depriving needy beings of the right to earn the bread honestly; Governments using technology to gain nuclear supremacy and bring humanity to collapse and that instead of spending millions to give health to so many children who they suffer from cancer and other illnesses, they take it upon themselves to destroy nations by maintaining an attitude of hatred and contempt for others. As an emissary coming from a planet where we have overcome everything the negative that is currently being lived on Earth, I, Higer, say as you say: You have to deal with your own shit. That's how I understood it (but they are not their words). As long as they do not turn their eyes to God, as long as they do not believe that they have a universal God of peace and love, they will be destroyed by their own pride. The Pleiadians and any being from another galaxy we cannot intervene in its evolution, everything is planned according to the purposes of God."

The message my teacher gave me was clear and definite. It is true that we are currently in a decadent society where moral value and respect for others is being lost. The people show too much arrogance and think that the material comes first; Instead of giving

God's love to their children, they are teaching them to Being selfish and envious, and they forget to be understanding and humble. From my personal understanding, beings from other planets see us as if we were in a divided zoo in cages as ferocious animals and not as rational human beings, where there is hatred, racism, and discrimination. Unfortunately, we men are currently finding ourselves in changes that are seriously affecting our planet Earth, I wonder if our governments are really capable of dealing with natural phenomena in the future, not far.

I personally doubt it, especially after seeing what happened with Hurricane Katrina; people are still claiming their properties that were damaged, and what can we say about other states that are being devastated here in the American Union by similar causes?

We cannot cover the sun with a finger and ignore that the changes obey prophecies already written in the Bible, which are summarized in the last times. I repeat: I do not speak for any religion, I simply try to make human beings aware of what is coming and precisely I was given the opportunity to send a message to prepare every living creature that is with expectant faith in him, that has lost trust in God, has suffered poverty, mistreatment, persecution, humiliation, and violations, and that he has been deprived of the right, as a human being, to share what others have given him.

Recently, at the beginning of the year 2007, I had the last divine revelation that deeply disturbed me and led me to write this book. I repeat that I don't know why they chose me if I can personally tell you that I made too many mistakes in my life. I know that God is gradually changing me, but as a human being I am not I stop falling into temptation or sin; I try to lead a straight life before the eyes of the Creator, but there is not a hair missing in the soup. Nevertheless, It is that divine fire that consumes me and tells me, "Do it, don't have fear of ridicule or ridicule. Speak for me and tell them what I think."This is how my Lord Jesus Christ spoke to me, "My wife was in the hospital and it was January. Everything was ready in the morning to take her to the operating room, she had to undergo a very big surgery, she had been diagnosed with ovarian cancer. We were on the ground floor of the sanatorium to prepare her while they gave us the authorization to transfer her to surgery. She was crying and very nervous. I remember her words before taking her away, she told me, 'Take care of our daughters, love them, and do not fight. Be patient with them.'

She talked as if she wasn't going to wake up and get out of the operation. I held back the urge to cry and told him that everything was going to be fine and that he had faith in God Our Lord. She asked me to please say a prayer, and so we both got to pray.

After a while the nurses arrived to take my wife to the operating room, I accompanied her as far as they allowed me, I kissed her, shook my hand, and told him to trust in God, to put himself in his hands, that he was by her side. Several hours passed and we were my sister-in-law and I in the lobby when the doctor arrived and told us that Mrs. Yolanda was fine, that they had diagnosed a cancerous tumor but that by doing the operation they had been able to see it was just an abscess. "This is a miracle," I told myself. I gave him thanks to the doctor and also to Jesús Bendito, who is great and merciful because my wife had come out of all danger; that's why she promised that I would bear witness to his greatness and his great love for everyone who believed in him.

After visiting hours, my sister-in-law went home and it was quieter. I got ready to go back to mine, but first I called to know how my daughters were and if everything was fine. They asked questions about when their mother was going to get out of the hospital. I had not told them about the surgery I had the next day so as not to worry them. The next day I told them that their mother had been operated on and they took it as normal, without surprise. I took the sanatorium for a visit so they could say hello to her mother. That night back home we were calmer, everything was normalizing. When I was already in bed resting, I thanked God the Father for his infinite goodness and mercy without knowing that this night would have a precious gift.

I was sound asleep when I had a wonderful visit: An angel of our Lord Jesus Christ appeared. I remember that in my vision it was day and that the angel of the Lord took me to a grandiose garden in which there were steps. He told me that the up and that when he arrived he would be in the presence of God Our Lord. I remember that I climbed too many steps, it seemed like an eternal climb, since when I finished ascending it was night, because he saw lights on the sides. It was then that I observed a hall too with a gleaming white marble floor, I felt the presence of angels guarding the place, I could say that it was the throne of God.

I heard a very cheerful young voice telling me, "Take off your shoes because the place you are stepping on is sacred." In an act of reverence, I obeyed and felt an aroma of incense and perfume that it was in the atmosphere. I heard again the voice that told me Come closer, don't be afraid. I felt an immense peace, I don't know why I perceived that there was a force that did not allow me to turn my eyes to see his face. I intuited that it was Our Lord Jesus Christ and, thanking him for my wife's recovery, for the miracle done, I told him,

"Sir, here I am, but why do I, being what I am, have

the grace that you call me before your presence if I am not worthy of you?"

"It is you whom I have called to serve me," she replied with a subtle smile. "I've been calling you; sometimes you answer me and sometimes you fail me, but it is me who now puts in your heart and in your soul the strength of the Holy Spirit so that with strength and bravely give a message to all mankind."

I fell into a state of laxity and my spirit began to have revealing visions. The message had two very strong calls; the first required that he speak to all who have suffered poverty and have gone hungry. He told me to go and tell his people that He, the Lord, affirms: "Everyone who has suffered for my sake I will reward. There will be no more crying or mourning, I will restore your health, the blind will see, the lame will walk and I will wipe away all the tears shed because of me My Father, in his Celestial Kingdom, has prepared an abode for each of you. Whoever believes in me will live forever and I will be his God, so I say! That's why now that he's close to my arrival, I tell you: Show your children the love of God, teach them everything good, that they love and respect each other and that they respect their parents, and that parents respect their children. I'm here and this time there won't be another opportunity, because the gates of the Kingdom of God will not be closed again. open, and all that is evil will be separated from that which is good, and the evil will be cast out into eternal fire!"The second call was for the people of God: Israel. Mr.

told me to go and tell his flock, "I will not listen to your complaints! even if they bump into each other like sheep at the Wailing Wall, a race of vipers! To all the churches I say beware of making each one of my children fall into sin because it is better for them not to have been born. I already have each of those so-called 'pederasts'! your punishment! To all those congregations that are exploiting the faith in my name profiting and saying 'thank God, I have all this' I already have theirs!" When I came out of my spiritual trance and was able to come back from my vision, I felt fear and dread. I heard the voice of our Lord Jesus Christ who, very upset, complained in a very strong tone. I felt a significant pressure in my chest and thought: How intense is the message of our Lord Jesus Christ, there is no doubt that God makes no distinction, he gives each one of us what he deserves.

That morning I went back to the hospital to take care of my wife, but I told her nothing about the vision or the calls to the people of God and to everyone in general. After visiting hours, I went home and prepared to rest. Higer introduced himself and told me that I could take the message to the media, I replied that I did not want to be a mockery of the public and that the best thing I could do was write it because that way the people who read me would believe and the ones who didn't, well that you don't believe I asked my teacher to help me with his intelligence so that this message would reach everyone and be on behalf of God, and so that no one would think that it is a story of a mind horny.

Higer told me, "Now that you know what the message of our Lord Jesus Christ is, it is time that you also tell all human beings why we are taking care of the Earth. But not we are in a visible form, we, the Pleiadians, are in the care of this planet by mandate of our Lord Jesus Christ, because the Earth is the dais of God the Celestial Father and the Pleiades constitute his throne, therefore, when the prophecies are fulfilled of time about the second coming of our Lord Jesus Christ, our act of presence here will be greater and greater."

The new message Pleiadean was received on January 4, 2022, given by the spirits superiors for the knowledge of the human race as a preparation for a new age, in which the acceptance of truth will no longer be hidden. Spiritualist doctrine speaks of its relationship with humanity, on moral laws, future life, and the future of humanity.

The teaching of the superior spirits deals with the scientific, philosophical, and religious aspects of God, the immortality of the soul, and the nature of spirits in relation to human beings and moral laws, I repeat, that was given through mediums, as Professor Allan Kardec, who suffered persecution and the burning of his books by the church, currently this philosophy is being known by all so that we have a superior knowledge about the laws of the universe, which Professor Allan Kardec (The book of the spirits) along with Xavier Chico, who was a medium and a writer spiritualist, he talked about aliens, which he mentioned in his book, that thousands of ships would gradually manifest from of the year 2022 on our planet.

My teacher Higer communicated to me telepathically about this new message, that according to the extraterrestrial brotherhoods, the beings that inhabit our galaxy, the Milky Way, and in our system solar, likewise the extraterrestrials that inhabit Venus and Ganymede, as well as the extraterrestrials of the star cluster of the Pleiades, Sirius, Orion, and other stars, as well as from the Andromeda galaxy and from other higher dimensions, will come to help us give a quantum leap and come to have a higher understanding with them, that allows us to get out of the darkness and approach towards the Christic light. Our Pleiadean brothers call the earth the planet "kinder," the conduit of this message is closed.

You must announce to them that when our Lord Jesus Christ arrives, it's not going to be like before when he was sitting on a burrito, but he will come like a thief in the night and one will be taken, and the other will be left. That is why you have to instruct every human being about the importance that within each family they reconcile and carry with harmony their life, that you await with pleasure and love the second arrival of our Messiah. His message is clear and definitive, there will be no other opportunity, He is going to take charge of taking the reins of his people while God the Father, with his angels, will take care of punishing all those who rebelled against him and against his Son."

Higer explained to me that when the time came for the Biblical and Mayan prophecies to be fulfilled, the planets of our solar system would align with the star Alcyone in the star cluster. star of the Pleiades. In the year 2012, Halcyon would be the throne of God and the light of our Lord Jesus Christ would be present. That was going to be the moment in which the Pleiadians were in charge of taking all the beings chosen by our Lord Jesus Christ, those who were faithful and pleasing to God. On the other hand, God the Father would be in charge of punishing here, on Earth, anyone who had rebelled against his Son and the Kingdom of God until he reestablished on Earth his footstool, for he will make the new Jerusalem.

After my teacher Higer's message, I felt more excited to pass it on through a book. Everything is to please Our Lord Jesus Christ. This is all that has been revealed to me, The rest is a matter of waiting with faith and love. There is very little time left let us take advantage of it in doing good, love God above all things, love our wives and children, trying to get by with everyone around us, which is difficult, but at least we must try it.

May the love and peace of our Lord Jesus Christ help us and

deliver us and keep us from all evil. Amen…The book shows a very clear message: The presence of our Lord Jesus Christ will make himself present to all humanity by fulfilling a promise he made to his disciples—and which extends to all one who trusts in Him—before ascending to Heaven.

The presence of extraterrestrial beings has always taken place in our lives. In the entire history of mankind, the fact that scientists and historians do not believe it is because we are living in a world where our intelligence is still limited because we are on an underdeveloped planet that is in the process of an encounter with spiritual hierarchies that will awaken all Human consciousness. When the time comes to face the end of the era, in the year 2012, gradually the Earth will be within what the Mayans call Tzab or the Serpent's Tail, which will begin with earthquakes and fires. He also talks about this Bible prophecy.

That is why it is necessary to wake up and believe that the events will come. We must be prepared to confront the wrath of God. Today we can say that the devastating earthquake in China opens the book of the Apocalypse of the Bible: The horsemen prepare to fulfill the prophecies while we wait for the arrival of the year 2012 when our star the Sun will align with all the planets and we will have the alignment together with the galaxy of Andromeda; The arrival of beings of light is also expected, which was present at the time of our Lord Jesus Christ as guardian angels.

This is according to what my teacher Higer has shown me in his Pleiadian teachings so that we are prepared to receive the messianic light from which every human being will have a direct confrontation with our Divine Master. That sparkle will engulf us, every human being will be healed and the face of the Earth will gradually be renewed according to its divine plan.

The Mayans and the Aztecs were instructed by their corresponding teachers, such as Quetzalcoatl, who brought great wisdom to Earth; They recorded that at the end of the ages, the human being will have a rapprochement with beings of light that will return from the stars to awaken in us a higher consciousness and a cosmic harmony, which will transform us.

Among other great researchers and psychics, Mrs. Alice Bailey mentions in her book Esoteric Astrology that "The Pleiades are the representation of the natural feminine and magnetic form of the Universe." As well as the famous archaeologist who discovered in the corridors of the great pyramid goddess the inscription that says, "His light from her is different to other lights, it awakens the answer. I am the densest point of everything in the concrete world. I am a tomb, also the womb. I am the rock that sinks by itself in the depth of the matter. I am the top of the mountain where the Sun was born, on which the Sun is seen and receives the first rays of light. Man takes a nature that is yours today, son of a mother born from the grave and showing after the birth the light." (Jesus Christ?).

Within the Inca culture, manuscripts were also found that say, "The stars are inhabited and the gods have descended from the constellation of the Pleiades."

If all cultures talk about the existence of the Pleiades and of gods or enlightened beings, why do historians insist on calling true history "mythology"? pyramids and the monuments on which the true truth is written origin of the cradle of our civilizations.

Gentlemen, it is time to wake up and get out of our ignorance, we are part of a universal proto-creation that tells us our divine origin, and that is why I find it stupid and arrogant that scientists put aside our Creator, putting us to the humans as primates.

Humanity still does not understand, do you want me to give you another sample of our arrogance and arrogance? On its opening day, Thursday night April 11, 1912, Titanic, the longest ocean liner largest in the world came to an end with a tragic collapse that caused the death of more than 1403 passengers, of 2206 who had addressed. The builders had called it "indestructible," since on her arrogant plaque was written, "Not even God the Father can sink it." And so I can write hundreds of tragedies on our planet.

I recently found an article that backs me up on my encounter with beings from the Pleiades star cluster, I was fascinated as they talk about the history of Cerro de la Estrella, which was unknown to me. The work goes like this: Huizachtepetl or Cerro de la Estrella, within the Nahuatl dialect, is located in the Iztapalapa delegation in Mexico City, in the Oriental. At the top of the hill, there is a pyramid where the Aztecs celebrated the ceremony of the New Fire and there are The remains of the ancient gods were buried next to the construction, according to data provided by the National Institute of Anthropology and History. Likewise, that precise place served as a setting for the public accountant, Mr. Enrique Mercado, to have an encounter with extraterrestrial beings on August 25, 1976. He mentioned that he was transported in the company of an extraterrestrial being by an invisible force that took him to an interplanetary ship and that he undertook an extraordinary and fabulous journey that lasted approximately 28 hours through stellar space, where he lived with men and women from other parts of the universe.

This interesting article is found on the Internet pages through OVNI TV, together with the article by Yohanan Díaz Vargas. There he says that every year in the famous Cerro de la Estrella they register many UFO sightings, especially when it takes place the celebration of the Passion and Death of our Lord Jesus Christ.

With this data provided by serious reporters and people contacted, I finish this book.

This Pleiadian message asks us to wake up and be prepared. My teacher of light, Higer, asks me to be the bearer of good news for humanity and that makes it reach all beings thinking of planet Earth. He said, "We Pleiadians don't We come to conquer planet Earth. We come to bring you the light and the love to bring out of the darkness all beings who wish to receive the cosmic philosophy of our Divine Messiah and Lord Jesus Christ."May peace and love reign among you. Amen…

The Pleiadian conduit closes.

About the Author

Agustín Osornio

After getting his high school degree, he opened his own business. He currently works as a commercial driver in Los Angeles, California.

After 20 years of marriage, he has three daughters. In 1976, his life changed when he was contacted by aliens from the Pleiades star cluster to be part of a highly advanced biogenetic experiment that scientists from Earth they do not know. The purpose is that it be a messenger who gives information about the future of our planet. The governments are leading everything to an irreversible collapse.

Until now it was ignored by the media, but Osornio cannot be silent: Through UFO. A message from the Pleiades shows how his extraterrestrial teacher gives him information about the future telepathically. In addition, he gives lectures on the extraterrestrial phenomenon; after the last one, in the parking lot, they told him to look at the sky. There they were—all those present could see the UFO that disappeared in a matter of seconds

www.ingramcontent.com/pod-product-compliance
Lightning Source LLC
LaVergne TN
LVHW041542060526
838200LV00037B/1099